☰string®

Modern since 1949. Thousands of new combinations yet to be discovered.

Summer

kindling
IMAGINATION

EDITOR IN CHIEF
Harriet Fitch Little

EDITOR
John Burns

ART DIRECTOR
Staffan Sundström

DESIGN DIRECTOR
Alex Hunting

ILLUSTRATOR
Espen Friberg

POSTER ART
Philip Lindeman

PUBLISHING DIRECTOR
Edward Mannering

ADVERTISING MANAGER
Jessica Gray

STUDIO & PROJECT MANAGER
Susanne Buch Petersen

DIGITAL MANAGER
Cecilie Jegsen

PROOFREADER
Julia Holzman

PUBLICATION DESIGN
Alex Hunting Studio

DESIGN ASSISTANT
Abbie Lilley

PUBLISHER
Chul-Joon Park

COVER TYPOGRAPHY
Pauline Fourest

WORDS
Allyssia Alleyne
Ellie Austin
Ariel Baker-Gibbs
Jennifer Barton
Jennifer Chen
Ed Cumming
Marah Eakin
Nell Frizzell
Selena Hoy
Robert Ito
Sarah Jaffe
Liz Kleinrock
Amil Niazi
Sarah Phillips
Robyn Price Pierre
Emma Scott-Child

PHOTOGRAPHY & STYLING
Gustav Almestål
Sarah Blais
Cayce Clifford
Andreas Frienholt
Linn Henrichson
Ruth Higginbotham
Sarah Hingley
Sammy Jackson
Suleika Mueller
Victor Pare
Julia Quante
Una Ryu
Emma Trim
Lisa Zomer

EDITORIAL BOARD
Jerrod Beck
Shanicia Boswell
Liz Kleinrock
David Michael Perez
Robyn Price Pierre
Emma Scott-Child

COVER PHOTOGRAPH
Suleika Mueller

ISSUE 03
Kindling is published
biannually by Ouur ApS,
Amagertorv 14B, 2, 1160
Copenhagen, Denmark. Printed
by Park Communications Ltd
in London, United Kingdom.
Color reproduction by Park
Communications Ltd in
London, United Kingdom. All
rights reserved. No part
of this publication may be
reproduced, distributed or
transmitted in any form or
by any means, including
photocopying or other
electronic or mechanical
methods, without prior
written permission of the
editor in chief, except in
the case of brief quotations
embodied in critical
reviews and certain other
noncommercial uses permitted
by copyright law.

The views expressed in
Kindling magazine are
those of the respective
contributors and are not
necessarily shared by the
company or its staff.

CONTACT US
If you have questions or
comments, please write to
us at *info@kinfolk.com*. For
advertising and partnership
inquiries, get in touch at
kindling@kinfolk.com

SUMMER and STORM

THE ANIMALS

OBSERVATORY

ISSUE THREE

Children's imaginary play can appear timeless. Cardboard boxes become racing cars; shampoo transforms into magic potions; kitchen brooms start to levitate. Without the high-tech toys that distinguish one generation from the next, even great-great-grandparents would recognize these scenarios and smile. For designer Cas Holman, however, imaginary play is so important because it's where the next generation sets change in motion. "If we're handed stories rather than getting to invent them, there's a status quo that comes with that. We become stuck," she tells Ellie Austin on page 72.

In the imagination-themed section of this magazine, you'll also find an investigation into how digital games can make space for creative thinking (quick takeaway: computers are not the enemy!) and another unpicking how the imagination fuels common childhood fears. In perhaps our most ambitious—and silliest—feature yet, we asked our Instagram community at @kindlingmagazine to send us descriptions of their children's imaginary friends, which the artist Linn Henrichson has brought to life through illustration.

Elsewhere in our third issue, we're interviewing Nadine Burke Harris, California's former surgeon general, about the long-term effects of childhood stress and trauma, and what can be done to mitigate them. In Berlin, Christine Sun Kim talks about the paucity of art pertaining to motherhood and the nuances of raising a hearing daughter as a Deaf woman. Although these circumstances are particular, her description of negotiating her daughter's increased independence without weakening their bond will feel familiar to many of our readers.

I wrote in our last welcome letter that getting to know our readers has been the most rewarding part of making this magazine. So, flick to the back of this magazine to browse Titbits—a new section full of short interviews with people raising children!

Editor in Chief
HARRIET FITCH LITTLE

COMMUNITY QUESTION

"My son is afraid of werewolves. Unfortunately, his middle name means wolf in Swedish. He doesn't understand transformations much— even Violet Beauregarde becoming a blueberry in *Charlie and the Chocolate Factory* freaked him out." (Mareka, The Netherlands)

WEREWOLVES

"My daughter is really scared of ghosts and she thinks putty marks on the wall are ghosts." (Mia, Sweden)

PUTTY MARKS

"When my oldest was about two, he was terrified of a violin we had hanging on a wall. He froze and screamed every time he saw it, as if he had seen a ghost. Eventually we had to put it in the basement." (Daniel, Sweden)

VIOLINS

"The *Peppa Pig* episode where George's dinosaur breaks!" (Stine, Norway)

BROKEN TOYS

"People knocking on the door. She prefers we just barge in. We tried knock-knock jokes a couple of times and it always ended up with her screaming 'Takut! Takut!' which means 'scared' in Indonesian." (Felicia, Indonesia)

KNOCK-KNOCK

What's your child's most unusual fear?

Thanks to everyone who shared their answers at @kindlingmagazine! Turn to page 90 for some insights into what scares children and why. TURN TO PAGE 90

"My son was terrified of loud automatic toilet flushes. He refused to go inside stalls at the airport." (Jill, USA)

TOILET FLUSHES

"My son checks his room every night for wild boars. My parents live next to a nature reserve where the population has exploded recently, and he's worried they will have run all the way from there to his bedroom... on the second floor of our house in the center of Antwerp." (Jasmijn, Belgium)

WILD BOARS

"Apparently there are giant, fluffy man-eating cats living in the ditches around our house called water gruff—they're a sort of gruffalo. We recently moved house so my son has been on the lookout for any new dangers in the area." (Nicole, USA)

WATER GRUFF

"My four-year-old is oddly fearful of freeways. When we're driving he asks 'Are we on the freeway now?' every five seconds. He normally loves anything fast but when it comes to freeways he would rather take the side streets!" (Erin, USA)

FREEWAYS

"My daughter thought I might be a witch, because I laugh like one. Once she even made up a story about how she thinks I turned her "real mom" into a parrot. It's funny, but concerning!" (Aiste, Lithuania)

MOM'S LAUGH

Part 1:
FIRST STEPS

ON THE COVER:
"The hats were on a different level!" says Jesuslina, who appears on the cover of Issue Three. Go to page 34 to see the full shoot.

Part 2:
BIG READS

46

REPORT:
THE SANDWICH
GENERATION

50

INTERVIEW:
NADINE BURKE
HARRIS

FEATURE:
THE FAMILY
ALBUM

62

34

FASHION:
HAT TRICK

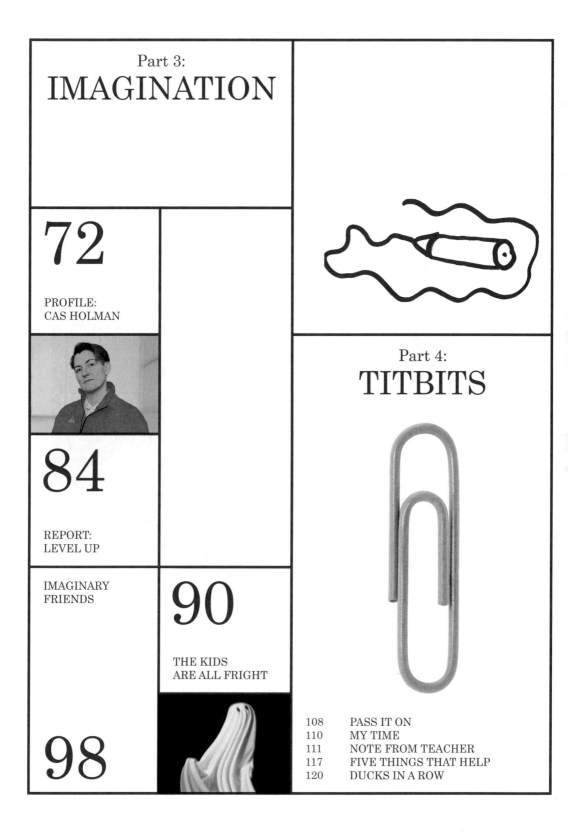

VIPP

V1 kitchen

A kitchen to last you a lifetime

Our steel kitchen is built to last. It will serve
you through thick and thin. Ups and downs.
If you are ready for a long-term relationship,
a Vipp kitchen is a perfect match.

VIPP.COM

Part 1:
FIRST STEPS

13 — 32

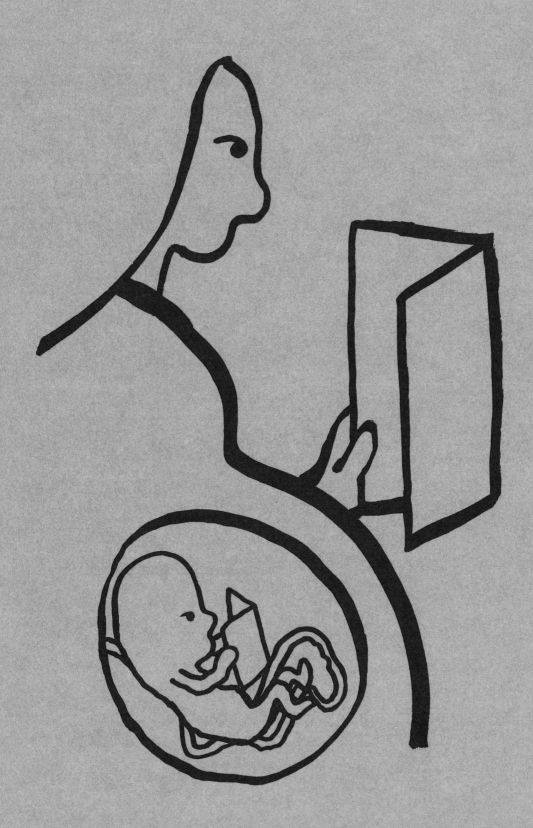

— **Book Smart**
Can progressive board books turn the page?

Words
AMIL NIAZI

One of the first purchases I made for my son as he aged out of board books was *My First Book of Feminism (For Boys)* by Julie Merberg. I was confident that it would be the perfect entry point for instilling a sense of equality and empathy in the son who I had convinced myself would be a daughter. I'm not alone. The appetite for progressive-themed books with titles like *My First Book of Protest* and *Stay Woke, Kids* has exploded in the last few years, as parents look to introduce concepts like social justice, anti-racism and activism to the next generation. Because of the demand for books on race following the murder of George Floyd in 2020, Penguin Random House tripled the print run of activist Ibram X. Kendi's board book for kids, *Antiracist Baby*. It's hard to attend a baby shower without seeing these books change hands—they are a particularly popular gift from people who don't have children.

On the first pass, I was devoted to reading every sentence of *My First Book of Feminism*. But I soon came to question some of the more didactic pages, ones that stated things like, "If you think strength means muscles, your thinking is wrong." My husband and I would look at each other and wonder: *Should we really be telling this baby his thinking is wrong?* He doesn't even know what a thought is. Eventually the book lost out to more exciting and fantastical journeys, to the words of Maurice Sendak and Ezra Jack Keats, to stories that centered children and their world, from their perspective.

Still, I persisted. I bought *Antiracist Baby* and many titles from the *Little People, Big Dreams* series which featured women like Maya Angelou and Emmeline Pankhurst, determined to find a child-friendly way to convey the ideals that I care about beyond modeling them in my everyday life. Unfortunately, most couldn't hold my son's attention. They weren't written with a traditional story structure and seemed sterile. They spoke *at*, not *to*, little readers. While the books were aiming for diversity, they missed a key part of representation: the ability for kids to imagine their way into awe-inspiring alternate realities.

This is not to say that children's books shouldn't grapple with these issues, in fact, they must. We read with our kids to inspire, excite and enthrall, to show them the vastness and possibility of the world they've found themselves in. Children can absorb lessons about empathy, activism and equality in many ways. For books to be a rewarding part of this journey, they must cater to their taste rather than those of adult readers. **k**

The boom in progressive board books has had many positive effects. For example, it has laid bare the biases and omissions in children's books more widely.

Few childhood memories are as cherished as the unexpected day off school. Sudden liberation is always more exhilarating than a long-awaited holiday. In places that are cold but not consistently so, the most common excuse is snow. In north London, where I grew up, my friends and I would head to the park and hurl snowballs at each other, laughing at the show-offs who brought their own skis. The teachers never seemed too unhappy about these days either.

Snow days are specific to a narrow band of temperate countries. Elsewhere, other types of weather can be just as disruptive. Friends who grew up in Canada and Sweden and Siberia, where snow is a fact of life for months of the year, didn't get a day off for a light fall. An ice storm might be a different matter. "Heat days," where it is too hot for schools to open safely, are becoming more common in the US and Australia. Southeast Asia takes precautions for cyclones, and schools close in the Caribbean in advance of a hurricane. It's not only the weather that can give children an unexpected day of freedom: Sinkholes, solar eclipses, spiders, bees and even, in Bangalore, a rogue leopard, have all caused closures around the world in recent years.

Yet one unexpected side effect of the pandemic might be the demise of this surprise reprieve. Earlier this year, New York announced that public schools would no longer have snow days. The students would be expected to work from home instead. They've proven they can, after all. In November 2020, a survey by the US-based EdWeek Research Center found that 39% of school principals had gone on to convert snow days to remote learning days as a result of their experience during the pandemic. The irony is that now schoolchildren have had a taste of home-learning—of spending all day, every day at home with their parents—they may not be so keen to stay home. A snow day is all well and good, but no school at all? It's no joke. **k**

In 2014, Reddit user Atrubetskoy crowdsourced data concerning the average snowfall required to shutter schools in different parts of the US. Below are some of his findings.

— Zero Chill
A eulogy for snow days.

24 inches

3 inches

Any snow

1 inch

Florida   Maryland   Northern Missouri   Alaska

Words
ED CUMMING

On "wine mom" merch.

— Bottle Fed

**Words
MARAH EAKIN**

In 2019, Jia Tolentino wrote in *The New Yorker* about "sassy mom merch" as a form of "quiet protest." As one mom told her: "When you put out a little signal on a shirt, like, 'I'm struggling too,' it starts a conversation."

When my twins were about to be born a few years ago, I thought I was prepared to be a parent. What I wasn't ready for was the stiflingly homogenous nature of mom-oriented merch and its apparent reliance on wine. Wine Mom culture is made up of merch and memes, often in swirling cursive, highlighting a reliance on wine to get through the day. It's not that these moms are always serious—making a joke about drinking at 10 a.m. on a Monday and actually doing it are two different things. It's often that they're overworked and underappreciated, and default to Wine Mom language as a way of voicing these feelings, with comments about "mommy's juice box" and seeking "liquid therapy."

I am not interested in the question of how much a mother should drink. Anyone looking for an opinion need only approach the nearest passer by, who will surely have one. But the idea that a mother's only respite from her often 16-hour workday is a big glass of cold white while her kids run screaming in circles around her is, frankly, depressing. Dads have their own stereotypical pastimes—references to grilling, fixing things and slinking off into "man caves" are all popular merch choices—but these activities at least suggest that they are allowed time to themselves. Moms are expected to hang in there and push down their struggles. In the past, women had sewing circles, mothers' groups or Tupperware parties to share their complaints. Now, we've got "I can't believe my kid" Facebook posts.

The idea that all moms love wine and/or that all moms are wine moms also ignores that, in fact, more than a few moms are sober moms, beer moms or weed moms—or maybe don't even like wine all that much. Though Wine Mom culture pitches itself as a big tent meant for all mothers, the reality is that it's tied to traditional gender roles most commonly found in straight couples. It is also a trope most common among white mothers who are reasonably affluent.

The old Latin phrase *in vino veritas* roughly translates to "in wine, there is truth." By contrast, Wine Mom culture seems to instead mask what's real, from the wealth and diversity of our experiences to our constant struggles to stay afloat. **k**

When kids and content collide.

— Sharenthood

The debate over digital privacy is as young as the internet, but raises evergreen questions about the conflicting rights of children and the adults who care for them. On the one hand, the United Nations Convention on the Rights of the Child states that "No child shall be subjected to arbitrary or unlawful interference with his or her privacy," and it isn't hard to see how—for example—an Instagram account dedicated to a particular child's experience of bedwetting misses the mark there. But parents and caregivers have a right to their own freedom of expression. They make decisions on children's behalf in many spheres already, and share information with friends and relatives as they see fit. Should the internet be treated any differently? **k**

42%

The percentage of teens who claim to be troubled by parents sharing information about them online, according to a 2020 Microsoft survey of 12,500 teens across 25 countries.

LIKE AND SUBSCRIBE

Online sharing can be lucrative. Although many "momfluencers" choose not to share details of their own children online, there is a currency to being open about one's family life: A 2019 Pew Research Center study found that YouTube videos featuring young children received three times as many views as other videos.

THE JURY'S IN

In 2020, a Dutch court ruled that a grandmother had to remove photos she had posted to Facebook of her grandchildren. The case was brought by the woman's daughter, who said she had not consented to her mother posting the pictures publicly. "With Facebook, it cannot be ruled out that placed photos may be distributed and may end up in the hands of third parties," the judge said.

72%

The percentage of US parents who say social media makes them feel less alone, specifically when it comes to behavioral issues, disabilities and postpartum concerns.

Words
SELENA HOY

Turn to page
119 for a list of
our sources.

FROM THE CRADLE

In the US, 92% of two-year-olds have an online
presence of some sort, with a third of those
appearing first as newborns or even fetuses.
One study from the UK found that the
average child had 1,500 pictures
of them online by the time
they were five.

31%

The percentage of parents
using social media who
have posed parenting
questions to their
online networks in the
last 30 days.

PETS AND PASSWORDS

On Instagram, 63%
of parents' public
accounts mention
their child's first
name at least once,
while 27% reference
their date of birth.
In 2018, UK bank
Barclays forecasted
that £670 million
(about $900 million)
of fraud could
stem from these
shared details by
2030. "It has never
been easier for
fraudsters to gather
the key pieces of
information required
to steal someone's
identity," Jodie
Gilbert, head of
digital safety for
Barclays, told the
BBC. The answers
to common security
questions—such
as the name of a
person's pet, or the
street they grew up
on—are often found
on social media.

FORGET ABOUT IT

Different entities have proposed different solutions. The UK's General Data
Protection Regulation includes the "right
to be forgotten" with particular provisions
for erasing data in cases related to child
protection. Meanwhile, Google announced in 2021
that anyone under 18 can request the removal of
images of themselves from image search results.

In a world run by children, garbage truck drivers would be top of the pay grade. My three-year-old nephew, Kazuma, lives each week in anticipation of Garbage Truck Monday and, last year, experienced the biggest thrill of his young life when local driver Adrian stopped to give him a toy garbage truck. I asked Kazuma what it is about the trucks that so fascinates kids his age. "They are big and green," he told me. "I love pickup trucks too!" Here are four alternative perspectives on the enduring popularity of municipal waste removal.

1. Most children cannot understand clock time until elementary school, but the garbage truck comes *like* clockwork—and often at a time of day when there is little else to get excited about. Amber Holly, mother of a six-year-old living in Seattle, says that routine is very important for her child. "Aiden likes seeing the same people every week. It's the same reason he likes the mailman. This was especially true during lockdown."

2. Even though the garbage truck may only come once or twice a week, garbage collection looms large in children's media. *Sesame Street* has not one but two characters dedicated to it: Oscar the Grouch, who lives in a trash can, and Bruno the Trashman, who picked up the neighborhood's waste for 24 seasons. Netflix has an animated show called *Trash Truck* about a six-year-old and his best friend, a giant trash truck, and a search in children's books on Amazon for "garbage truck" brings up over 2000 results.

3. Young children are intensely interested in how and why things work. "Garbage trucks are big and noisy and have big visible mechanical processes; either the compressor of old that crushed the trash in the back, or the lift that dumps the can over the top. It's easy to grasp their workings," explains André Alyeska, a mental health worker in Oregon who was captivated by the trucks as a child. Kids revel in the noise, too, in a world where they're often shushed. "They have great sounds you can mimic later in pretend play. *Vrroom, errrr, crrrush,*" says Alyeska.

4. Children start to develop pretend play around two to three years old. At the same time, they start to form friendships. When a garbage truck driver is happy to acknowledge or even interact with the kids on their route, it's no wonder children become smitten. "When my son was two years old, his dream was to drive the garbage truck through town," remembers Ruthie Iida, owner of a children's English language school in Tokyo. "We lived in an apartment complex, and he would follow after the truck on pick-up days, puffing and panting as the truck drove slowly from apartment to apartment. The guy who rode on the back of the truck would smile and wave to my son as the truck chugged along." **k**

Some authorities have issued guidance on how kids can greet the garbage truck safely. According to Alaska Waste, you should "make eye contact, wave, and make sure the driver is aware that you are approaching."

— Trash Talk
Why do kids love collection day?

Words
SELENA HOY

— On The Couch: Mrs. George

Mean Girls, but a good mom.

High school is tribal. The cult status of the movie *Mean Girls* is based on its sharp skewering of this fact. Alpha Regina George and her followers, the Plastics, oversee their dominion of hormonal, insecure teens at North Shore High School. Newbie Cady Heron, who's been homeschooled by zoologist parents in Africa (the country is never specified) quickly learns that, just like lions, the students prowling the halls know exactly where they stand in the social hierarchy.

While most teen films would have us believe there are no more cliques once we slam the door on high school, *Mean Girls* also dives into the divisions within modern motherhood. On the one hand, you have Cady Heron's mom: a "hands-off" working mom. She's a highly successful academic who's been offered tenure at Northwestern University—it's her job that prompts the family's relocation to Chicago.

Then there's Regina's mother, Mrs. George: a well-off stage mom type. "I'm not like a regular mom, I'm a cool mom," she proudly asserts when meeting Cady for the first time. For Mrs. George, "cool" motherhood translates to being fluent in teenspeak, adopting a "no rules in this house" attitude and attempting to be BFF with her daughter's friends. Her suburban stay-at-home uniform—a pink Juicy Couture tracksuit with a teacup dog tucked under one arm—is taken straight from Paris Hilton's early aughts playbook.

Mean Girls came out in 2004 and these characters must be viewed through the lens of '90s "mommy wars" feminism, where stay-at-home moms were constantly pitted against those with careers, a debate which regularly played out on the pages of magazines, in books and on TV. These two supposedly binary "choices" were weaponized by politicians in larger cultural debates of the era.

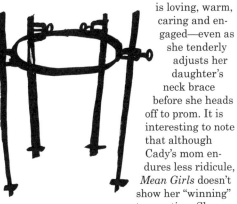

On first viewing, Mrs. George has all the attributes our society condemns in mothers: She's superficial, youth-obsessed and totally chill about letting her tween daughter Kylie mimic the flashing spring breakers of *Girls Gone Wild*. But look deeper and you'll see that Mrs. George is, in fact, a good mom too. She embodies the "everything under my roof" parenting style teens wistfully long for. Refreshingly sex-positive ("You guys need anything? Some snacks? A condom? Let me know!"), she understands that teens will experiment. As she explains to Cady when offering her alcohol, "If you're gonna drink, I'd rather you do it in the house."

A lot of parenting happens behind the scenes, without an audience, yet in *Mean Girls*, we repeatedly get glimpses of Mrs. George in these moments. She's enjoying herself, happily snapping pics and recording videos from the sidelines. She is loving, warm, caring and engaged—even as she tenderly adjusts her daughter's neck brace before she heads off to prom. It is interesting to note that although Cady's mom endures less ridicule, *Mean Girls* doesn't show her "winning" at parenting. She is out of the loop when it comes to the struggles Cady is facing and willfully naive to the predatory nature of high school politics.

Mean Girls takes our prejudices about certain mom "types" and upends them. Mrs. George ultimately (and unexpectedly) emerges as committed to doing the best for her kids in a society where mothers are judged no matter what choices they make. At its heart, *Mean Girls* is a movie about finding fulfillment in ourselves regardless of how others choose to perceive us. Mrs. George perfectly encapsulates this sentiment, and isn't that *so fetch?*" **k**

Mrs. George's sex positivity is in conflict with her daughter's school, where students are told that if they do have sex, they will "get chlamydia... and die."

Words
JENNIFER BARTON

Brief answers to big questions.

— Great Question!

> Question
> from an adult:
>
> HOW CAN I GET
> MY CHILD TO
> REALIZE I'M A
> PERSON TOO?

A baby, we know, recognizes people as a distinct category. Your child is aware that you are not a dog, nor a spoon. But the bigger question is how we get a child to recognize the *value* of our personhood. How can you explain to someone who relies on you to meet their most basic needs that you are not a free-floating extra limb?

"Language acquisition is a really significant moment in which the world becomes divided into 'me' and 'other'," says UK-based psychotherapist Fia Lindley-Jones. "Before then, children are probably in a synesthetic world where touch and color and taste are all fluid and all interlinked. Then you have a word [for example] for 'mother' or 'me' and that changes the perception."

When children have language, use it. "It's useful for your children if you can name your humanity," says Lindley-Jones. "To say: 'I'm feeling very tired because I didn't sleep well last night and that means I'm low on patience so, when you say that, I feel upset.'" That's in an ideal world, of course. More likely, you will get upset and they will see it, but in verbalizing why and explaining what you're doing to make yourself feel better, you can highlight your own feelings, while also modeling

Words
NELL
FRIZZELL

for your child how to recognize theirs. Be prepared for the relationship to fluctuate. "When a child is in a state when they most need their primary caregiver, they will go back to believing you can read their mind," says Lindley-Jones.

Finally, remember that the emotions your child is feeling are not all that different from your own, and that both are changing all the time. "Most of us know the ambivalent feeling of not wanting to leave your child while also desperately wanting time to yourself," concludes Lindley-Jones. There will be times when handing your child over to another adult will feel like pulling your heart out of your chest. There will be times when you will want to run for the hills. The more open you are in your emotions, the better your child will come to understand that you, like them, are a person. Not just a hairy spoon. **k**

Question from a child:

WHY ARE YOU SO OLD?

Few of us like to think of ourselves as old, let alone "so old" as to elicit comments from a child. But talking about how you got to be the age you are can be a plus for both of you. Maybe you haven't thought about all of the advantages that come with being older, or even full-blown *old*. And there's a decent chance the child hasn't either. According to several studies conducted over the past half-century or so, school-age children already have the same sorts of ageist attitudes as the rest of us. In the eyes of the young, old people are weak, slow, ill-tempered, impatient, needy, less physically active and less able to deal with stress. They're also apparently uglier and less healthy, more prone to sitting and generally less fun as playmates. No wonder the question stings! But adults aren't all bad. Kids do tend to view youngish adults as smarter and more competent than they themselves are, and older adults as warmer. Questions about age are a good chance to talk to your young friend about what it means to be old, and what they think it might be like. As long as you don't gas on and on about how much better the good ol' days were (they weren't) or how much easier kids have it nowadays (they don't), they'll listen.

What does "so old" mean to a kid anyway? Depending on the age of the child, there's a good chance that they don't really know how old you are, not really, particularly relative to other things. Until the age of six or so, kids are still wrestling with the difference between yesterday and tomorrow, past and future. Many of them can't really distinguish between something that happened 20 years ago and 80, or tell the difference between someone who's 50 and another person who's 70. For a lot of kids, anyone over 40 or so may have ridden to middle school on dinosaurs, so don't take it too much to heart. **k**

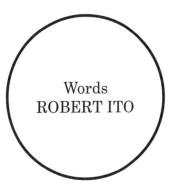

Words
ROBERT ITO

It Changes Things:

CHRISTINE SUN KIM [born **1980**] is an artist living in Berlin where she makes work about how sound operates. In **2017** she gave birth to a daughter, Roux. She tells *Ariel Baker-Gibbs* about how motherhood changed her art and what it's like to raise a hearing child as a Deaf woman.

Christine Sun Kim was born in 1980 to Korean immigrant parents in California. Mostly working with interactive multimedia installations and charcoal drawings, she explores language, power and sound through works such as *Face Opera ii* (2013), in which Deaf participants perform operatic scores of visual expressions without using their hands. She is fascinated by visual representations of data and uses them to express different facets of the Deaf experience, shown in her pie chart series *Degrees of Deaf Rage* and her 2020 exhibition *Trauma, LOL* at the François Ghebaly gallery in Los Angeles. Her more recent works demonstrate her interest in questions of public visibility and delve into her Korean American identity and experience of parenthood.

Christine Sun Kim is sitting at her table in Berlin wearing a black puffer jacket when we meet on Zoom. The connection is not perfect and we have to pause and wave our hands every now and then to check we're both catching everything. Kim signs quickly as she jumps from thought to thought, often reenacting memories and sharing examples. Even the moments of emotional intensity are grounded in laughter, especially when her daughter Roux gets home from school and wants to play.

ABG: You're a Korean American Deaf artist raising a hearing child in Germany. How do you think about the ways her childhood will differ from your own?

CSK: I've been thinking a lot lately about the Korean term *gyopo*. It essentially means "red-blooded." It's a slightly pejorative term meaning "not really Korean," like an outsider—but it's been reclaimed as a more positive identity.

My grandparents were forced to leave North Korea and moved to America with their children. And then I moved further east around the globe to Germany. And now I wonder, will Roux stay, or will she move further along the globe back to Korea? That'd be funny, but I think about gyopo and what it means. What ties us together through diaspora? What are roots?

My mom is the eighth [child] in her family and my dad has five siblings. I have almost 40 first cousins in America.

When Roux was born here in Germany, I looked at her and realized: She has no cousins. She is hearing. German is her first language. ASL is a close second. So little of her experience here is related to being around Deaf people or to being Korean, and that scares me. I want to give her that direct experience, to have her be just a little bit like me.

"I THINK A LOT ABOUT WHAT ART AS A MOTHER COULD LOOK LIKE."

ABG: How have you worked to build those connections?

CSK: We brought Roux to the US last summer. She was glum the whole time. She felt like an outsider because she didn't have much English. But when we went back for Christmas, she was so happy being with my parents and my Deaf sister. So I can see it takes some effort to calibrate her sense of Korean American identity. I'm still scrambling to make sure Roux has Korean or half-Korean friends like herself.

ABG: Your work tends to center on language, play and the processes of hands-on and visual investigation—all of which are so precious to Deaf people because they're hard-won. I see you thinking about these things as Roux acquires

language and becomes her own person. What's her relationship with language right now?

CSK: Roux is about to start at an international school with bilingual instruction in German and English. She's been at a bilingual daycare with DGS (Deutsche Gebärdensprache, or German Sign Language) and German. It's a good program, and the Deaf teachers are wonderful, but the program is run by hearing people and I can sense a distinct hierarchy between the hearing and the Deaf teachers at that place. I don't want Roux to pick up on that. Recently, she acted out a story about a bird who laid an egg and she told me "The egg is hearing." I asked, "Why not Deaf?" And she said, "Because hearing is better." It was clear. The system is just too much at work. So it seems just as well for her to start the new school—she needs English anyway.

ABG: How do you approach these questions of language at home?

CSK: Sometimes I think, wow—she is so *hearing*. Tom, my hearing partner, is really good at following the rules that we use sign only at home, no voices. Before, we had said if I was in the room with them we would sign, and if I wasn't in the room they could use their voices with one another, but we realized that doesn't work so well. So now they only sign at home even if I'm not there and use their voices out in public. But sometimes when we're out, I'll realize Roux is talking

Previous: Christine wears a shirt by Jil Sander and a coat by Christian Wijnants. Left: She wears an outfit by Closed. Overleaf (left): She wears a shirt by Essentiel Amsterdam and a blazer and skirt by Ganni. Overleaf (right): She wears a shirt by Jil Sander, a coat and trousers by Christian Wijnants and shoes by Ganni.

"SO LITTLE OF HER EXPERIENCE IS RELATED TO BEING AROUND DEAF PEOPLE OR TO BEING KOREAN, AND THAT SCARES ME."

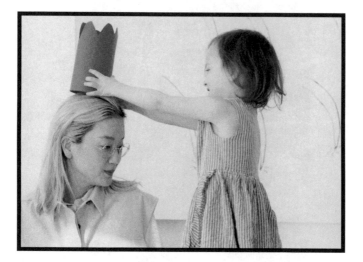

to a hearing person and that I don't know what they're talking about at all. I'll ask what happened and she'll tell me. But sometimes she doesn't see why she should. We still struggle to frame it in a way that works, that respects her independence but also includes Mom.

It's exhausting as a mother and as a Deaf person. Just the amount of energy you give as a mother is compounded by that extra tension, and to come up against these dynamics within my own family is really hard. Occasionally I break down, at other moments it's just fatigued annoyance. I sometimes wonder, why do I put myself in these situations that I constantly have to massage to make it work?

ABG: Much of your art is for Roux, about Roux or has Roux contribute to it. To what extent has she inspired your work?

CSK: After Roux was born, I made *Sound Diet*. I pretended I was a doctor prescribing

amounts of sound, like Netflix or Spotify or whatever. I wrote them down using my own system of musical notation. That and *A Week of Lullabies for Roux* were the results of me being preoccupied with how much Roux absorbed auditorily. I wanted to be more conscious of what she consumed.

During the pandemic, we also did a project together making a coloring book. She would come into the studio and play with the art supplies and make messes, and leave behind some pictures that I just really liked. But now she's more aware of boundaries: She'll look at me and ask for permission, and I'll invite her in. I recently designed a gyopo sweater for the Lunar New Year with four tigers drawn by the four generations of my family—my grandmother, my mom, me and Roux.

ABG: How do you imagine this relationship will evolve as she grows up?

CSK: I want to make sure there will always be room for Roux in my work. I want her to influence me as much as I might influence her. It could be because the lack of systemic support depletes mothers, or because women are generally less regarded in the art world, but I feel like art about motherhood just isn't very well documented. I think a lot about what art as a mother could look like. And I feel like art itself is an opportunity to get Roux out to see new things. I love it when her eyes narrow and her mouth sets, like she's thinking, forming her opinions. She's completely her own person. **k**

To sign "mom" in ASL, open your dominant hand and touch your thumb to your chin.

Part 2:
BIG READS

33 — 70

HATTRICK.

Left: Elizabeth
holds two baseball
caps featuring the
KINDLING mascot
Claude, which
were made for
this photoshoot.
Previous:
Jesuslina wears a
KINDLING bucket
hat and a sweater
by ARKET.

Jesuslina
wears shorts by
SUNCHILD, a hoodie
and sandals by
BOBO CHOSES and
a KINDLING
bucket hat.
Jesuslina says one
highlight of the
shoot was working
with hair stylist
Sammy, who she has
known since she
was a toddler.

BOBO CHOSES

Jesuslina wears
a sweater by
MINI RODINI,
shorts by
SUNCHILD, sandals
by BOBO CHOSES
and sun hats
from AMAZON.

Elizabeth wears
a T-shirt by ARKET
and a KINDLING
bucket hat.

Jesuslina wears a
sweater by ARKET,
shorts by WYNKEN,
shoes by BOBO
CHOSES and a hat
by EGG TRADING.
She says the shoot
was "just like a
day out."

Elizabeth and
Jesuslina wear
sweaters by ARKET
and KINDLING
bucket hats. Both
girls say that
taking photos
together was their
favorite part of
the day.

Jesuslina
holds a KINDLING
bucket hat.

Elizabeth wears a
hoodie by JELLY
MALLOW and a hat
belonging to Ruth,
the stylist.

Elizabeth wears a
sweater and shorts
by BOBO CHOSES and
hats by SUNCHILD
and KINDLING. She
says this was her
favorite outfit
from the day.

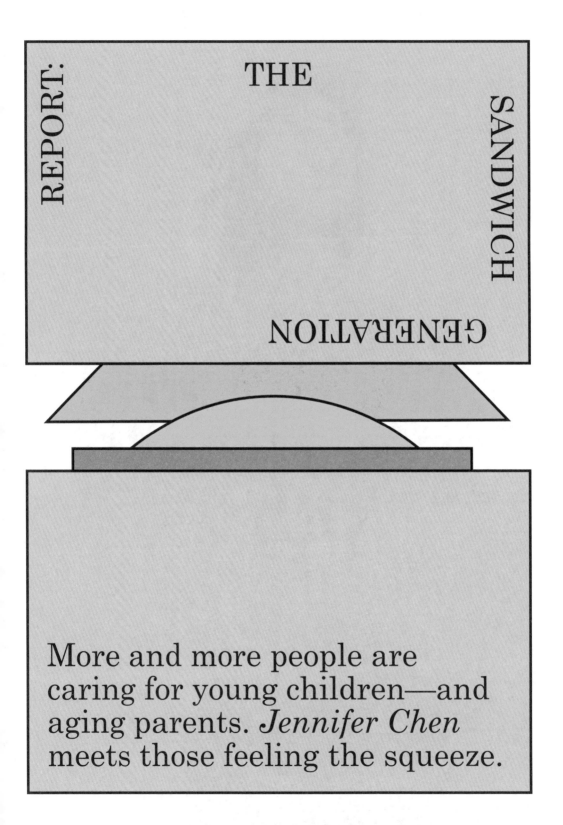

REPORT: THE SANDWICH GENERATION

More and more people are caring for young children—and aging parents. *Jennifer Chen* meets those feeling the squeeze.

"Relief and self-loathing" is how author Helen Hoang described the emotions she felt after her mother passed away in an essay for *Oprah Daily*. The novelist and mother of two had been providing end-of-life care for her mom, a Vietnamese refugee in the US, who had lung cancer. Hoang relied on her husband to care for their own children while she and her older sisters provided round-the-clock care for their mother.

"I didn't give myself self-compassion when my mother was ill," Hoang tells me over email. "I did what I thought I was supposed to—push myself to my limits and keep it up as long as possible—and I believe this is why I experienced such a difficult depression/burnout after my mom passed away." Her latest romance novel, *The Heart Principle*, closely mirrors her real life. Her main character, Anna, tag-teams hospice care with her sister and mother for a father with cancer. Hoang credits the writing process with providing much-needed relief. "I was so used to keeping silent and hearing what other people thought of me," she says. "Through the power of storytelling, I was able to not only explain but show everyone what it was like to walk in my shoes."

Hoang isn't the only one experiencing the crushing squeeze of managing both the care of aging parents and dependent children. Christened the "sandwich generation" by American social worker Dorothy A. Miller in 1980, this growing group of people, predominantly women, are often working full-time while providing physical assistance and financial support to the generations above and below. In the UK, a 2013 report found that a quarter of adults had provided this form of "sandwich care" at some point in their lives.

Not all intergenerational caregiving is taxing; it has the potential to be mutually enriching. Picture the family where active grandparents help raise young grandkids, and then those same grandkids, now older, help care for their grandparents as they age. Perhaps this family lives together in a house that offers space for both communal gathering and privacy. Perhaps there is additional support: a wider network of relatives living nearby and state-subsidized care workers available when necessary. In the US, 82% of multigenerational households report that living together has enhanced their bond.

But these cushioning factors are hard to come by, particularly in Western cultures without a tradition of

According to Pew Research, 12% of US parents have a child under 18 living at home while also providing care for another adult.

"I didn't give myself self-compassion when my mother was ill."

community-based care. And demographic factors have knocked things out of sync. In the United States, women with a college degree or higher, on average, give birth around age 30—much older than new mothers in the early 1980s, who first gave birth at age 23. At the same time, people are living longer. In the US, the 85-and-older population—the group that requires the most care—is projected to more than double from 6.6 million in 2019 to 14.4 million in 2040. Whereas previously a person's children might have been teenagers or even have left home by the time their parents became infirm, they are now caring for still-young kids and assisting aging parents at the same time.

The pandemic has stretched the sandwich generation even thinner. In 2020, as schools, daycare centers and elderly care services shut down, many families took on full-time care responsibilities. It was during the pandemic that the term "caregiver burnout" gained currency when referencing healthcare workers who have tended to waves of dying patients around the world. Many of the same problems apply to people caring for children and seniors in a private capacity. Typical symptoms for caregiver burnout are similar to signs of depression: withdrawal from friends and family, irritability, a feeling of hopelessness and physical exhaustion. In certain cultures, like Hoang's Vietnamese family, self-sacrifice for elders and family is seen as a badge of honor. It can be hard to address your needs if you think they aren't as important as the needs of a sick parent or young child.

Caregiving requires an exorbitant amount of time and energy. A Gallup poll in 2011 revealed that employed caregivers looking after elderly people typically spend 13 days per month on day-to-day tasks like grocery shopping, transportation and laundry. They also spend around 13

The phrase "triple decker sandwich generation" refers to people in their 60s who are caring for both parents and grandchildren.

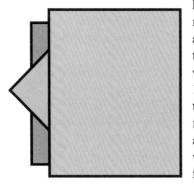

hours each month on financial matters, scheduling doctor's appointments and administrative tasks. Add in the fact that working mothers spend around 11 hours a day on tasks related to child-rearing (stay-at-home moms average 18 hours a day), and it's no wonder that the sandwich generation has no time for themselves.

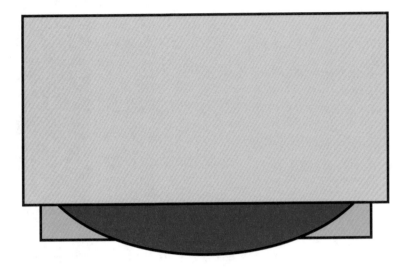

During the height of her burnout, Hoang shares that though she was physically healthy, she wasn't able to function like she normally does. She found herself being more clumsy, unable to remember things, easily distracted and having intense feelings of anguish. "Mental health is just as important as physical health," says Hoang. "For people who find themselves in similar situations, I can't adequately emphasize the importance of self-advocacy and communication."

Typically touted self-care practices, like a massage or a day off, may well be impossible for people who are caring for others. What might work instead: asking a friend or family member to give you a few hours off, talk with a close friend, or seek a local support group or therapy. Hoang recommends repetitive-type hobbies as being potentially soothing—puzzles, coloring books, exercising and gardening.

But this squeeze won't be resolved through self-care. Employers should be more flexible with work hours and remote work. Childcare and eldercare should be more affordable and easily available. Relying solely on individuals to shoulder the burden of being sandwiched between parents and kids is a recipe for constant stress and anxiety. For Hoang, finding peace in the meantime meant being kind to herself. Writes Hoang: "And for my readers who are facing similar challenges in their lives, I hope I give them a voice. They're not alone, and they should not feel ashamed if they're hurting. They're not 'less.' They're human, just like I am." **k**

WORDS: ROBYN PRICE PIERRE

na
ad

Dr. Nadine
Burke Harris
will see you now.

For California's former surgeon general, stable childhoods are key to happiness — and longterm health.

In 2007, Dr. Nadine Burke Harris was an early-career pediatrician working in the underserved neighborhood of Bayview, San Francisco, when she met a seven-year-old who would set her on her life path. The boy, Diego, was small for his age and had asthma, eczema and behavioral problems. In conversation with his mother, the doctor learned that he had experienced assault as a four-year-old. Burke Harris, who had long suspected that stress could impact health and development, was struck by a thought: *"Wait a minute. Is this seriously enough to cause a child to stop growing?"* Today, she leads the field in researching adverse childhood experiences—ACEs—and the impact they can have on long-term health outcomes.

Between 2019 and early 2022, she also served as the first surgeon general of California, where she championed health equity, introduced screenings for ACEs across the state and helped launch a $4.4 billion program to support behavioral health initiatives for children. On top of that, she helped shepherd the state through the health crisis of the century, COVID-19. Earlier this year, Burke Harris took the lessons she has been teaching about self-care to heart when she announced her resignation from the office to look after herself and spend more time with her husband, four sons and bucolic garden.

Burke Harris uses the hanging nest in her garden (pictured right) as a space for meditation.

The garden sits
atop a hill, and
is a haven for a
wildlife. Cayce,
our photographer,
saw a lynx walking
through some
grape vines.

RPP: How did you come to study childhood adversity?

NBH: It came naturally from going to practice in this underserved community where I was hearing the same stories
over and over again among my patients and seeing how
that was affecting their health. That's what drove me to
dive into the science about how early adversity affects children's health and development, how it affects their brains
and bodies. Then, in doing that research, to also recognize
that we didn't really have a lot of systematic solutions.

RPP: Can you introduce the concept of ACEs for readers not
familiar with the term?

"I don't think there's any family that has been
    spared hardships, or difficulties, or struggles."

NBH: The 10 traditional ACEs include physical, sexual and
emotional abuse, physical and emotional neglect, as well
as growing up in a household where a parent experienced
a mental illness, substance dependence, incarceration,
where there was parental separation or divorce, or do-
mestic violence. ACEs are strongly associated with an
increased risk of negative health outcomes.

Initially, people thought if you have ACEs, you are
more likely to do all the things that increase your risk
for disease. You're more likely to drink and smoke, for
example. What we now understand much more clearly is
that when you experience an ACE, it activates your body's
stress response. And when the body's stress response is
activated too intensely and too frequently, and you don't
have adequate buffering or caregiving, it can lead to pro-
longed activation of the stress response. That is what we
now call the toxic stress response.

RPP: Can you talk about the culture of silence surrounding childhood trauma and adverse experiences?

NBH: Silence is a huge part of the problem. When Dr. Vincent Felitti, the principal investigator for the study on ACEs, first proposed doing the study, people were like, "No, you can't ask patients about this, they'll become unraveled, they'll commit suicide." So, he carried an emergency pager 365 days a year—any patient who had answered the ACE questions, he had to be available to them.

RPP: It can be a scary thought for an adult that, because of factors outside of their control when they were children, they are at greater risk for major health issues. What can people do?

NBH: Things like yoga, mindfulness, meditation and regular exercise help us to metabolize our stress hormones and release healthy hormones, like endorphins. Also, nutrition, mental health and healthy relationships.

RPP: Healthy relationships?

NBH: Yes. Healthy relationships are one of the most powerful antidotes to an overactive stress response.

RPP: It's impossible to insulate children from all stress. You talk a lot about the power and scientific benefits of buffering—can you tell me a bit about that?

NBH: I'll tell you what it looks like for me personally as a parent. It's taking that time to just connect and tune in to your child. Just kind of listening, and saying, "Hey, what's going on with you?" And your child doesn't have to be a baby, it's whatever age they are right now. I don't think there's any family that has been spared hardships or difficulties or struggles. Recognizing when kids are experiencing or witnessing that, and giving them the opportunity to tune in and be cared for, sometimes means reaching out to your extended family. And that's certainly been true in our family. I pat myself on the back. I'm a darn good mom. But my kids are not going to get everything from me, right? And so, they have relationships with their uncles, aunties, grandparents, coaches, teachers and the other people in their lives who create that ecosystem of care. It takes a village. It's a cliché for a reason: Having as many people as possible recognize how they can be a support to kids who are struggling—and breaking the cycle—is really important.

There is a lot that can be done to combat the impact of ACEs, but "it requires us to talk about it," says Burke Harris.

RPP: Toward the end of your book, *The Deepest Well*, you turn to your personal experience of how trauma shapes us. You write about the loss of your baby boy, Ziggy, who

Burke Harris'
self-care regime
is distinctly
West Coast: 4.30
a.m. starts for
journaling,
meditation,
exercise and an
oxygen mask. "If I
were to do it in
the evening, there
are so many ways
that it can be
interrupted."

died in the hospital minutes after he was born. Where are you on the journey of processing this loss?

NBH: When a mom loses a child, it's an entirely visceral experience. It is the worst agony I have ever experienced in my life. It took me a while to even realize that I was lost. It was my brother looking at me and saying, "Are you okay?" and my saying, "No, I'm not okay," that it kicked in. I was like, "Wait a minute. I know what to do." When we're in our lowest moments, we're just gasping for air, we're just trying to put one foot in front of the other. And when I realized I wasn't okay, in a way that was such a relief because I know what to do when someone is not okay.

RPP: What are some of the things you did?

NBH: I knew I had to do all the things that I know work. This is what I do for a living. I knew I needed support. Someone needs to support our kids. Someone needs to take care of me. I meditated twice a day. I went for a walk for an hour and a half a day. I took time off work. I connected with people who love me. I was regularly seeing my therapist. Every year on our son's birthday, we plant a tree. I feel so much peace around it, and so much healing. Getting to cram a whole lifetime's worth of motherhood into 14 minutes—I feel grateful for it. I feel grateful for having had the experience of being his mom. I would never wish the loss of a child on anyone, but now it's a very meaningful experience. It took a lot of work.

> In *The Deepest Well,* Burke Harris writes that "even bootstrap heroes find themselves pulled up short by their biology."

RPP: When you resigned from your position as California surgeon general, you said it was to prioritize care for yourself and your family. I thought that was extraordinary—especially from someone in your position—to honor your needs like that.

NBH: My job requires extraordinary focus, and so it was important for me to listen to myself and recognize that I feel proud of what we've accomplished; *and* I also know that it's important for me to take a break. My taking a break and taking time to rest and connect with my family and myself and my group of social support is an investment in my future work.

RPP: What are you going to be doing now, with so much time on your hands?

NBH: I'm gonna be spending a lot of time in my garden. k

In her farewell speech as surgeon general, Burke Harris said she was proud of her part in the pandemic response because it allowed "kids to have more time with their grandparents, spouses to have more time with their partners and mothers to have more time with their babies."

WORDS: ALLYSSIA ALLEYNE

THE FAMILY
ALBUM

The pleasures and pitfalls
of making music
for children.

On a video call from her home in Brooklyn, Elena Moon Park, artistic director of the music-making nonprofit Found Sound Nation, is recounting how she first came to perform with the Grammy-winning children's music ensemble Dan Zanes and Friends, back in 2006.

"The first show I ever played with Dan was the best musical experience I've ever had in my life," she says. "Kids are such an honest and beautiful audience, so it was an incredibly different experience for me in terms of playing music."

Born to South Korean immigrant parents in east Tennessee, Park grew up playing the violin, but had always felt unsure about a career in classical music, which suggested staid audiences in rarefied concert halls. Playing for families and children, though, has provided an alluring alternative. Where playing classical music felt "very removed from people," Park says, playing for families with children felt like a shared experience. "I fell in love with it immediately."

Park would go on to tour the world with Dan Zanes and the ensemble as a multi-instrumentalist until 2012, performing inoffensive folk-rock for the under-10 set. In 2017, she released her own children's album, *Rabbit Days and Dumplings*, a whimsical collection of children's and folk songs from East Asian countries including Korea, Japan, China and Tibet.

In doing so, she joined the much-loved but critically overlooked world of adult musicians who have dedicated their lives to making music for kids.

Children's music is one of the only markets where the targeted demographic has little say in its criticism, purchase or creation (see also: music for pets, plants and fetuses). This means that musicians must pull off a balancing act of surprising complexity: They must charm their diminutive listeners with simple lyrics and catchy melodies, without driving the grown-ups in their lives up the wall.

From the awarding of the first "best recording for children" Grammy in 1959, to the high-pitched debut album from Alvin and the Chipmunks, artists from many different walks of life have taken up the challenge. Ella Jenkins, dubbed the "First Lady of Children's Music", studied child psychology and worked as a youth program director at the Chicago YWCA before moving into children's entertainment; Robert Lopez and Kristen Anderson-Lopez, the married composers behind the eight-times platinum *Frozen* theme "Let It Go," made the leap to Disney after making their names in musical theater. (Lopez won Tonys for his decidedly more mature scores for *The Book of Mormon* and *Avenue Q*.)

But children's music often seems to be something people fall into rather than aspire to create. In his 1999 autobiography *The Life of a Children's Troubadour*, Canadian singer-songwriter Raffi, possibly the most famous children's performer of all time, wrote that he was barely making ends meet as a folk singer, "singing to inebriated audiences who couldn't care less if I was there or not," before an invitation to perform for students at a local school set him on the path to stardom. Likewise, Greg Scelsa and Steve Millang, who've performed educational songs as Greg & Steve since the 1970s, were wannabe rock stars working as teaching assistants for special education classes before they decided to perform for kids full-time. ("It certainly beat

A song such as "Baby Shark" works well for children, but infuriates adult listeners. As Jimmy Kimmel quipped, "Whoever is responsible for it should be locked in prison for the rest of their lives."

playing Holiday Inn bar gigs," Scelsa told *The Los Angeles Times* in 1994.)

Music critic Stefan Shepherd, who has been reviewing kids' music on his blog *Zooglobble* since 2004, believes a similar opportunism may have contributed to the spike in adult artists releasing children's albums shortly after 2006, a bumper year in which three albums aimed at kids topped the Billboard sales chart: the original *High School Musical* soundtrack, followed by *Kidz Bop 9* and *Sing-A-Longs and Lullabies for the Film Curious George*, the latter by Jack Johnson. "I think there were some artists who were like, 'I'm not having the success that I want to see in the adult field relative to sales or critical acclaim or whatever,' and saw this kids' field as another way [to succeed]," he says. "Some of those albums weren't very good, but some of the artists were like, 'Oh, wow: I actually connect with this audience better than I did when I was playing in bars,' or for whatever reason [found that] making music for kids just fulfilled them creatively and helped them live their lives more easily."

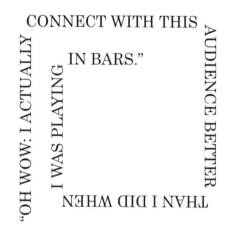

"OH WOW: I ACTUALLY CONNECT WITH THIS AUDIENCE BETTER THAN I DID WHEN I WAS PLAYING IN BARS."

But there have always been players from other streams dipping their toes into the kiddie pool—from Johnny Cash,

What do Ray Charles, One Direction, Cher and Erykah Badu have in common? All have appeared on *Sesame Street* to sing children's songs.

Saint Etienne and Ziggy Marley to André 3000 and They Might Be Giants. These are names that mean nothing to kids but might appeal to adults who want child-friendly songs from artists they already enjoy. "If you're a fan of a band, and you grew up with them, and then all of a sudden you turn 32, and you've got a three-year-old kid, and that band makes an album for kids, that's mind-blowing," says Shepherd. "It's a way to share my favorite band with my daughter."

By the same token, it's often parenthood that first prompts musicians to write for children. It was only after the birth of his first son in 1970, after all, that Johnny Cash applied his rich bass-baritone to songs about magic glasses, dinosaurs and why the number one is no fun.

Walter Martin, who played in New York rock outfit The Walkmen from 2000 to 2013 before launching a successful solo career, credits his daughters Claire (now eight) and Louise (now nine), with his decision in 2014 to release a children's album *We're All Young Together*, which included duets with Karen O and The National frontman Matt Berninger. "I've never had any desire—or ability—to be an actual children's entertainer or anything," Martin says from his home in upstate New York. "I was initially drawn to the idea of making a kids' record because I liked the idea of doing it as a kind of art project. Like, what would my fantasy kids' record be like? I really made it for myself and for my kids and I was honestly very surprised that it got so much attention and kind of launched the chapter of my career that I'm still enjoying." He now has three more kids' albums under his belt.

Composing music that will appeal to both kids and parents is an art in itself,

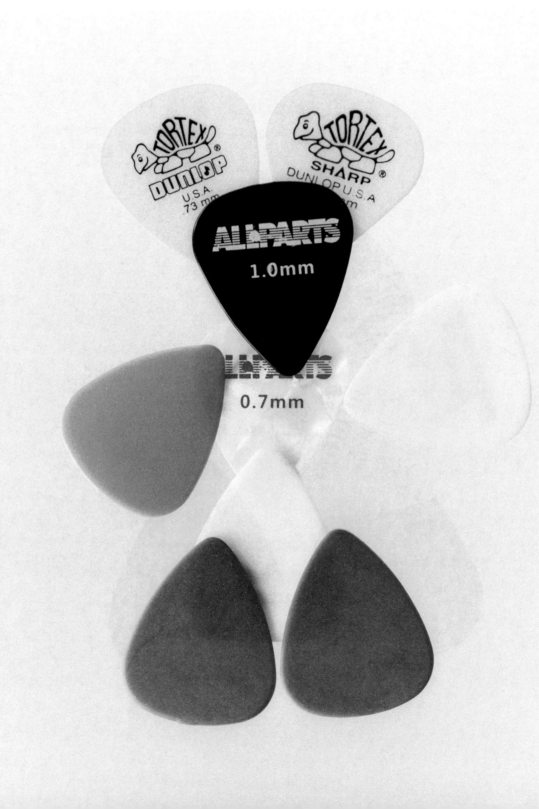

and for Martin, this is one area where having a live-in focus group has been especially helpful. "When [my daughters] were littler, and before they discovered Ariana Grande and Lizzo and people like that, they would listen to my songs a lot. I'd play them stuff I was working on to see if they liked it. Kids have a pretty intuitive reaction to good beats and good melodies so I could judge if something was working or not based on their reaction."

While children's music itself ranges from uptempo playtime music to quiet lullabies, getting the subject matter and lyrics right is particularly important. There's a fundamental difference, Shepherd explains, between a song kids can enjoy, and a song written for them specifically. "The Beatles are great but they're not singing for four-year-olds," he says. "I think people may find it challenging to get into the mindset of a kid and think about what kids are interested in."

When it comes to lyrics, for Martin, the difference between writing for kids and adults is the same as the difference between talking to each group. "When I talk to kids, I'm basically the same as when I talk to adults, but I'm maybe a little lighter and friendlier and I don't use bad words or talk about death or existential dread, and maybe I make more dumb jokes," he says. "But I'm still myself and I don't use funny voices or baby talk, and I certainly don't talk down to kids." As adult listeners, we're likely to judge the success of these albums by whether they can be genuinely enjoyed or merely endured. But, even if our favorite kids' album is reviewed on *Pitchfork* (it happens), or its maker profiled in longform in *The New York Times* (ditto), a kids' album seems only ever to be cool in an interesting way rather than an edgy or avant-garde way.

Not that it matters much to those making it. For Elena Moon Park, success is measured by the audience's response to the music itself. She recalls the number of times she's had the parents of Asian kids express their appreciation for her modern renditions of traditional Asian songs or watched her nieces perform her music back to her.

"You know, anytime you just see kids having fun and enjoying the music, it really warms your heart," she says. "I think if you connect with one person in a performance, or even if you and your musicians on stage are enjoying the communal act of playing music together, that is a successful performance in my mind." k

"IF YOU'RE A FAN OF A BAND, AND THAT BAND MAKES AN ALBUM FOR KIDS, THAT'S MIND-BLOWING. IT'S A WAY TO SHARE MY FAVORITE BAND WITH MY DAUGHTER."

JOHNNY CASH
Colombia Records, 1975

WALTER MARTIN
Family Jukebox, 2021

JACK JOHNSON
Brushfire Records, 2006

Part 3:
IMAGINATION

71 — 106

WORDS: ELLIE AUSTIN

cas

No rules. No repetition. No "right" way.

A toymaker's
tools for
better play.

Cas Holman doesn't consider herself a toymaker, despite creating objects that keep children occupied for hours. Instead, she describes her job as "designing for play, imagination and education." It's why her best-known designs—Geemo, a system of flexible magnetic branches; Rigamajig, a 265-piece, oversized construction kit; and Imagination Playground, a series of blue blocks and shapes each as large as a child—don't come with instructions. There is no right or wrong way to engage with Holman's play objects; the goal is for them to nudge children to think freely and collaborate with others.

"I worry that we overprogram children's days and we give them ready-made stories," she says when we meet at her Brooklyn studio, which is full of shelves stacked with books and toys made by herself and others. Holman's two dogs, Wiley and Knuckles, sit calmly at her feet. "It's always in the interests of keeping them occupied, but if we're handed stories rather than getting to invent them, there's a status quo that comes with that. We become stuck. You can design for consumption or participation and I consider my work a success when I see kids make something with it that I never would have thought of."

Holman has dedicated her career to designing for children because she believes "good toys make good people."

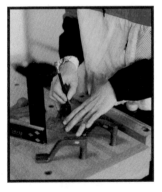

Holman's desire for children to be the architects of their own play stems from her childhood in Northern California. Her mom was a Montessori teacher and weekends and evenings were spent "in the woods, building a house out of a bush," or helping her stepdad—a mechanic—in the garage. She remembers her school days, however, as a disheartening web of rules and rigidity.

"I was irritated that I had to be still and be inside," she says. "We're taught to behave in this way that isn't human. I saw that people around me were being serious because they felt they had [to be]. I thought, *That's a game and maybe sometimes I'll play that game if I have to.*"

Her disinterest in conforming to gender norms added another layer of frustration. In the Netflix docuseries *Abstract: The Art of Design*, for which Holman was profiled in a 2019 episode, she explains how, when clothes shopping as a child, she always longed to choose items from the boys' section. Today, she doesn't necessarily believe that all toys should be unisex but rather that, regardless of their gender, children should be encouraged to "dress up in a tutu and play with a tool kit." "Let's allow kids to play with gender and teach them to engage in a whole spectrum of play," she says.

"I consider it a success when I see kids make something that I never would have thought of."

After high school, she enrolled at the University of California, Santa Cruz, but dropped out when she didn't get the first-year grades to continue as a scholarship student. Following a break from academia, which included a stint working for her aunt and uncle at a research center in the Galápagos Islands, Holman began an M.F.A. in 3D design at Cranbrook Academy of Art in Michigan. It was here that she found her professional footing.

"That was when I started sketching more as a way to communicate ideas," she says. "When I sketch, my hand becomes an extension of my brain and they're going back and forth."

She designed Geemo while at Cranbrook and, a couple of years after she graduated, it went on sale at the MoMA Design Store in New York. By this point, she was working at the city's Rockwell Group design firm, helping to prototype Imagination Playground, a collection of large-scale, blue foam blocks, chutes and cylinders that children can assemble however they want. The playground debuted in 2008 to widespread acclaim and was adopted by UNICEF as part of an initiative to give children in developing countries access to open-ended play. Its success convinced Holman, who until recently was an associate professor of industrial design at Rhode Island School of Design, that there was an appetite for new thinking around what constituted positive play.

Holman also works on larger scale projects, such as her recent design for Movescape, a playground on the roof of a New York community centre.

Holman recently
moved her
studio from
Rhode Island
to Brooklyn,
and with it
her eclectic
collection
of inspiring
objects.

BIRD
MILL

BIRD MILL

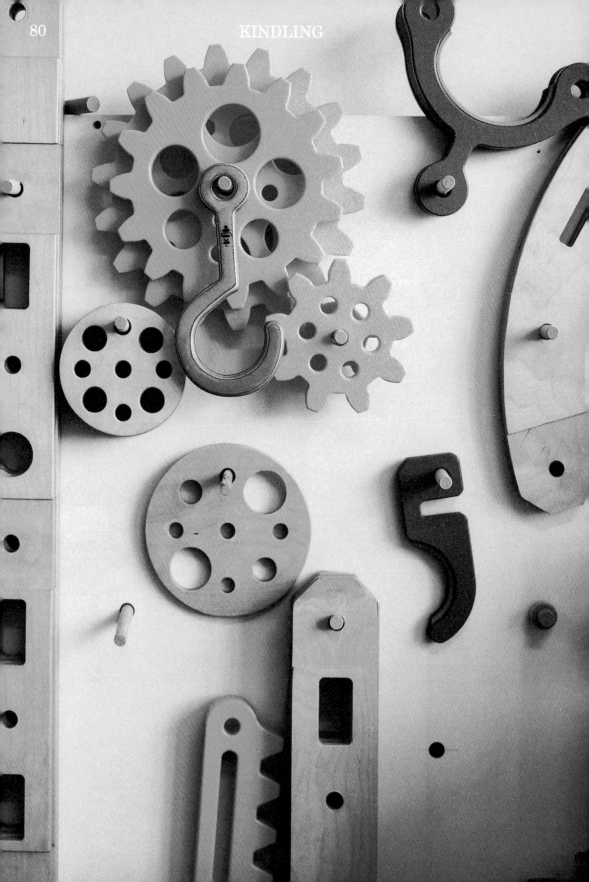

"Toys from decades ago are really occupation-based," she says. "You'd give a child a tiny sewing machine. The message was that they were just killing time until they were adults and able to work. What if we prioritized messages like, Are you happy? Are you getting along with other people? As cultural artifacts, toys say so much about how we understand children at a specific time."

Today's mainstream toys, she explains, signal that we've reached "peak capitalism" in our approach to childhood. "A lot of popular toys have batteries that you can't change because the makers know you won't need to. The child will be done with the toy before the battery dies. I don't think we respect children and that's visible in that we give them things that can't be taken care of."

Rigamajig began life in 2011 as a pop-up playground on New York's High Line. Next came three years of reimagining its wooden planks, wheels, nuts, bolts and pulleys for mass production. During this time, Holman sought feedback from teachers and children. What notes did the

kids give her? "They'd say things like, 'Why doesn't it fly?' or 'It should be made of ice cream!' I'm like 'You're right, it should be!'" she says, laughing.

There is a steep price barrier to actually owning Holman's play objects. A Rigamajig builder kit costs $3,865, and is really intended for purchase by museums, libraries and classrooms rather than individual families. She has worked hard to ensure that her creation doesn't simply end up in spaces that are already well-appointed, partnering with corporations and charitable foundations that pay to send kits to public schools in underserved communities.

However, she is adamant that the ethos of unstructured play need not rely on access to deliberately designed

To understand how children are using Rigamajig (pictured left) Holman often joins children in play. On one recent museum outing, she helped build "an island for mermaids and giraffes."

objects and advocates for the joy of "found materials," such as empty water bottles, yesterday's newspaper, a plant pot or an old pair of socks. "There's a common anecdote that the box the toy comes in is more popular with kids than the toy itself and that's true because, with the box, the child gets to contribute to its story," she says.

Recalling a recent incident with the child of a friend, she emphasizes the role of parents in fostering imagination. "This little guy, he'd got a Lego set and put it together as a town and a gas station. I said, 'Let's take it apart and see what else we can do!'" she says. "Then his mom came in and said, 'You're not going to be able to put it back together right.' I said to her, 'Let's talk about that. What does it mean to be right?'"

"Let's allow kids to play with gender and teach
        them to engage in a whole spectrum of play."

Similarly, Holman believes that, as we emerge from the pandemic, children will be taking cues from the adults around them as to what constitutes "safe" play. "Right now, kids have an impulse not to be near one another and that isn't going to change without us actively saying, 'It's okay to ask that child next to you for help,'" she says.

There's a common perception, she explains, that she's an all-out critic of screen time for children—but that isn't the case. "I'm not a Luddite," she says. "I do think some digital play can be positive." Such as? "There's this lovely app called Windosill. It starts as a blank screen and children can build their own imaginary journey. It resonates with what I do because it lets you participate in the concept." (The app describes itself as equal parts puzzle game, physics toy box and living picture book.)

A common refrain of Holman's when explaining her commitment to her work is that "Good toys make good people." Are there telltale signs in an adult that they were encouraged to play freely and imaginatively as a child? "They never actively forget how to play," she replies, "and they know how to integrate play into conversations so that, when conflicts arise, they figure them out with imagination. We all have an imagination and sometimes it's fun to share but we also need to show kids that being alone with your thoughts can be wonderful." **k**

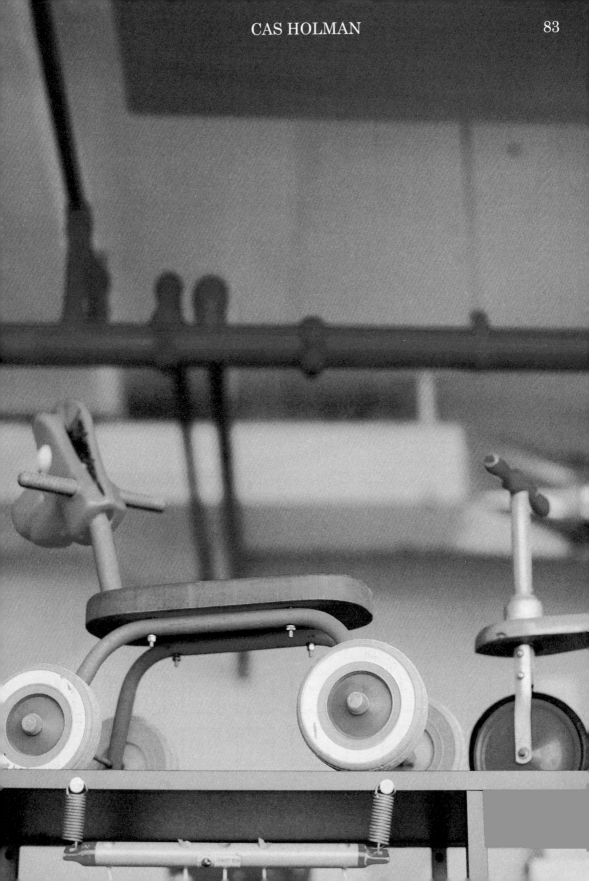

Can digital games make room for big imaginations?

Today's kids are digital natives. My 16-month-old son is a lockdown baby who is as familiar with video calls as he is face masks. When his four-year-old sister started school last year, she was immediately signed up to an app to enhance the learning experience.

In many aspects of life we accept the utility of these interventions. But what about at playtime? There is a rose-tinted image of what young children's play "should" look like: cardboard boxes converted into rockets and elaborate castles fashioned out of sheets and chairs. Digital play is harder to romanticize and involves fewer beguiling props. The picture conjured is of children who are engrossed but not engaged, their faces illuminated by blue light, a meltdown looming on the horizon if you even think about suggesting a screen break.

This concern isn't just borne out of nostalgia, or the transference of our own anxieties about technology addiction. Play can be divided into various interlocking subcategories, each with its own pleasures and developmental benefits. Social play, for example, teaches children how to cooperate, while physical play improves motor skills, strength and fitness. For a child's imagination to flourish, "free play" is particularly important: unstructured time in which the child develops ideas and desires in any direction using the tools available. Digital games, particularly the early rudimentary ones, find it hard to deliver this—they are often governed by strict rules, goals and time limits.

But the digital realm is now packed with companies looking to create innovative new outlets for imaginative development. Chris Lindgren is a play researcher who was one of the first employees at Stockholm-based app company Toca Boca, which prides itself on making digital games that nurture young minds. "Compared to games where you might have limits or collect points, and on the other side educational apps, child-led play wasn't really present at that time," Lindgren says of the gaming landscape in

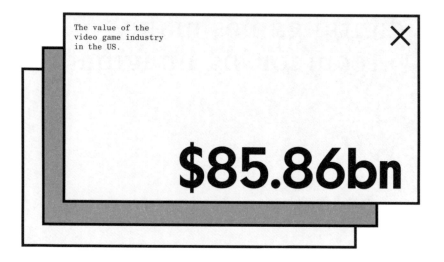

```
The value of the
video game industry
in the US.
```
$85.86bn

"Imagination begins from birth.
Children understand their place
in society through play."

2005, when the company was founded. She and her colleagues wanted to do something different: "It was about pure play."

Toca Boca's Helicopter Taxi, which allows young players to simulate flight—something that even the wildest of imaginations could never achieve—was released in 2011. Since then, the market for make-believe-based digital games has exploded. Nowadays kids are often at the control panel of their online adventures, able to do everything from composing music for cartoon animals to dance to (in Loopimal), directing animations (in Fox and Sheep's Movie Maker for Kids) and even coding their own stories with apps like ScratchJr.

Lindgren spent a lot of time observing children and was constantly surprised by how they responded to what was on screen. "They really wanted to explore the limits, especially small kids," she says. When trialing one game, she recalls: "Kids wanted

to put several hats on top of each other on characters we had and that was not supported. But we understood we had to support it because it was so crucial to their play." When some mini testers came to the office at the time of the Eurovision Song Contest, they were adamant that a plant in the game needed to be able to dance and sing.

"Imagination begins from birth," says Professor Lisa Kervin, director of Early Start Research at the University of Wollongong. "We see how children understand their place in society through the way that they play." For a study conceptualizing digital play, Kervin identified apps where the child is "able to manipulate objects and take on new perspectives" but which are not focused on winning or losing. What Kervin's team found highlighted many positive and unexpected uses of digital play for feeding creativity. For example, one family she spoke to had taken their son for a haircut

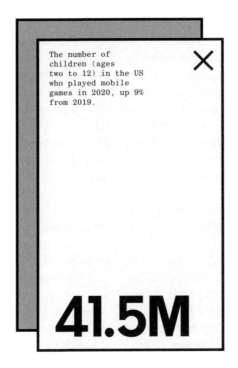

The number of children (ages two to 12) in the US who played mobile games in 2020, up 9% from 2019.

41.5M

and he insisted on bringing his iPad along, which his parents presumed was to play with. But when they got there it emerged that he wanted to show the stylist how to cut his hair using a salon game.

The boundaries inherent to digital spaces are often mentioned as a reason why they are less stimulating to the imagination. Think, for example, of how Toca Boca adapted their games according to feedback from children: They can program a plant to sing according to one child's whims, but what happens when another child comes along and wants it to ice skate? But this question is not as unique to the digital realm as it might seem. As the Soviet developmental psychologist Lev Vygotsky has noted, children often restrict elements of play themselves based on the social norms they are aware of, for example in role-playing games like pretending to be doctors or babies in which they mimic the conventions of real life.

In digital play, the inverse often happens: Rather than creating rules in the manner observed by Vygotsky, kids find imaginative ways of breaking them. Fiona Scott, a lecturer in digital literacies at the University of Sheffield, says she has been struck by the ability of young players to manipulate a digital platform to do what they want. In Animal Crossing, she says, they often "build their own community around a specific aspect of how you could play the game, not necessarily following the storyline or trying to achieve all the goals." Scott thinks that digital play can provide real freedom to explore creativity. "Traditional play specialists, like Dorothy G. Singer and Jerome L. Singer would say the best toy a child could have would be a cardboard box, because of the imaginative possibilities," Scott says. She points out that digital "sandbox" games such as Minecraft, which allow the user to build their own world, are not that dissimilar. "Children are empowered to experiment to do things differently." Scott has an 18-month-old daughter who is already able to take photos on a phone. "It doesn't mean that we don't do finger painting as well. But it is another way to engage with the world, creatively and imaginatively." When she reads books to her daughter that involve a pig, she likes to show her a video of the animal to enhance the experience.

This sort of hybrid play is increasingly common, not least in the ingenious ways that technology has been adopted by children during the pandemic. The UK's Play Observatory project has documented the Zoom birthday parties, Skype craft activities with grandparents and online board game sessions that became part of the fabric of childhood in recent times. There are some particularly inventive ways of making digital play communal, as Scott explains: "On YouTube, there are videos that are designed to show what different rollercoasters around the world are like. In one of the families we observed, this was really important to them. They would put cushions down on the floor, sit in front of these videos and ride the rollercoasters." Philip So, a toy designer based in Canada, has worked with app developers Sago Mini and the ABC network to turn their characters into physical toys. Of watching kids during testing he says: "You knew you were onto something if they would get fixated on it and then try things out. Maybe [they would] start off playing with it the way you intended or perhaps they would go in a totally different direction."

Children will always find ways to play, whatever the circumstances and tools available. Perhaps our concern over their use of digital spaces stems from our own limited imaginations when it comes to technology: There is much more to a screen than the infinite scroll. "We could all use a little bit more play," says So. Who says it is just for kids? **k**

"Small kids really want to explore the limits."

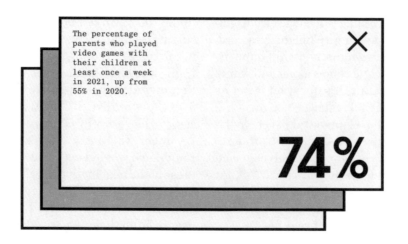

The percentage of parents who played video games with their children at least once a week in 2021, up from 55% in 2020.

74%

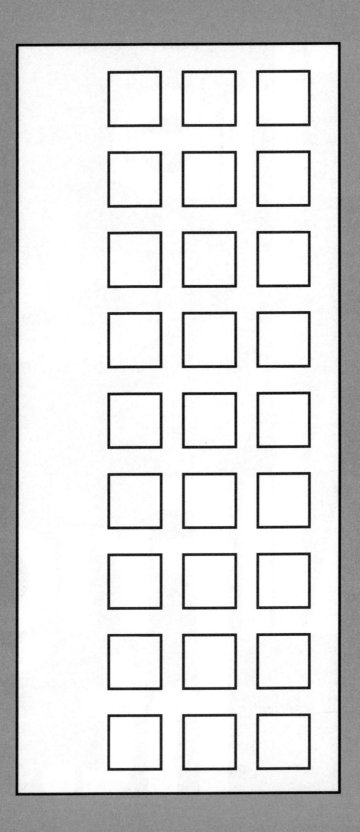

WORDS: SARAH JAFFE

The Kids Are All Fright.

What
makes
something
scary to
a child?

The finality of death is scary, but many of the scariest creatures that the human imagination can conjure are those that blur the line between living and dead: zombies, spirits and ghosts. Dr. Carolyn Kessler, a Brooklyn-based licensed child psychologist who has been working with kids and families for nearly 20 years, explains that, while most six-year-olds can imagine a ghost lurking in the corner, that's not the same as actively fearing it: "Where the anxiety comes in is more in how reactive they are to their thoughts. Most kids can *imagine* that something may be hiding under their bed. A subset of kids will have reactivity to that idea, where it becomes a more interfering fear." A child who imagines that every creak of the floor or whistle of the wind is a ghost may become too nervous to sleep alone. Dr. Rachel Busman, a clinical psychologist at Cognitive and Behavioral Consultants in New York, suggests that children can gradually build up their tolerance to being alone and learn that nothing bad is lurking to get them: "In the case of worry related to sleeping alone, we might start by having a child go into bed and stay there for 15 minutes before a parent checks on them. The child would do that for a few days and then we might extend the time to 20 minutes and so on."

(PREVIOUS) GHOSTS

CLOWNS

Everything from a mall Santa with a fake beard to a person wearing a balaclava can be scary to children. Clowns, with their exaggerated features and odd-looking makeup, can be especially terrifying. "Kids fear things that interfere with their sense of safety," explains Dr. Kessler. A child can't identify a safe or familiar person whose face is hidden, whether by a scary Halloween mask or even a friendly-looking one. In the book *Monsters Under the Bed and Other Childhood Fears*, psychologists Stephen W. Garber and Marianne Daniels Garber note that a fear of hidden faces, masks or people in costume is common among preschool-aged children, ages three to four.

METEORS

The idea of a catastrophic event that's completely unforeseen can be extremely scary to kids once they're old enough to appreciate the devastation that natural disasters can cause. Emy, who lives in Brooklyn and is the mom of a six-year-old son, had no idea when he picked up a nonfiction children's book about meteors at the library that it would set off a fear that would last for months. The book stated that astronomers have identified and are tracking 95% of near-Earth objects, but Emy's son didn't find the statistic comforting. "That seemed particularly concerning, as that means that 5% of near-earth objects have not been observed yet and could come to earth without warning," Emy says. The ability to understand natural phenomena, including the unpredictability of weather disasters or meteors, usually happens in early elementary school and can lead some children to fear those aspects of the natural world. Dr. Kessler says that, even though she and her clients live in Brooklyn, where tornadoes are rare, she's worked with numerous elementary school-aged children who are scared of tornadoes. "They're afraid of the disaster that might happen," she says. "I can give them the information, but I can't guarantee them that it won't happen, because these things do happen."

Being afraid of something requires a certain capacity to imagine a negative outcome and an ability to project into the future. As our brains and imaginations develop, so do our fears. Lots of things can make a kid anxious about sleepovers: being out of their typical routine, being in a new place—and that's before you even get to the classic sleepover activities, like telling ghost stories. Most kids won't host or attend sleepovers before mid-to-late elementary school because younger children are often fearful about being separated from caregivers. However, though that fear dissipates throughout childhood, older children "show more worries in relation to their peers and the perceptions people have of them," Dr. Busman explains. Being at a sleepover makes things that are usually private—what your pajamas look like, whether you sleep with a stuffed animal—into public information, and can ignite fears of judgment or scorn. A kid with the ability to imagine being made fun of, or that something bad will happen if they're the first to fall asleep (or the last) might find themselves dreading an activity that's supposed to be fun.

SLEEPOVERS

CLOSETS

Closets don't usually hide anything other than clothes or junk, but a child can imagine that far more sinister things might be lurking in there. One Brooklyn-based mother, Robin, recalls hearing an urban legend when she was seven years old about a murderous doll who came alive in a closet, opened the door, and killed a whole family. In an unfortunate twist of fate, Robin's father came home from a business trip a few days after she'd heard the story and brought her a new doll, which was stored on the top shelf of her bedroom closet. That confluence of events made her imagination run wild and set off a multi-year fear of closets. "Every night, part of my ritual was 'Is my closet door closed?' I wanted to make sure that the door was closed, because that would stop the doll from coming out and killing everyone in my family," Robin says. Fear of dark rooms, closets or of something lurking under the bed is one of the most common childhood fears; *Monsters Under the Bed* lists "dark" as a fear that can start at age three and last until age 12.

THAT

We asked *Kindling* readers to describe their children's imaginary friends, then *Linn Henrichson* brought them to life.

SPOOKY GHOST CRAB lives in London, where he lurks in the shower at three-year-old Kit's house.

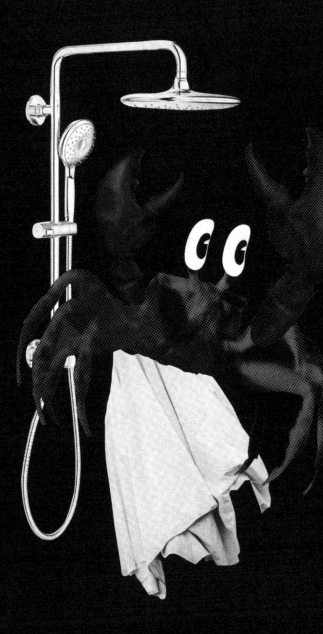

This imaginary friend doesn't get up to much. "He's just a spooky ghost crab who likes sitting in the shower," says Kit's mom, Sarah. "Kit's three and a bit limited on words but ghosts are big—he likes pointing them out watching us from corners." She reports that Kit liked Linn's rendering of his friend: "Eyes! Spooky crab!" he said.

LE LOUP is a light-fingered wolf who lives with two-year-old Isla and her parents in Lyon.

Isla's imaginary friend is always stealing things, from the living room sofa to her brother Ryo (who, luckily, was returned minutes later). Isla's dad, Kiel, says that Le Loup is sometimes nice, but often naughty. "Isla insists that she is not at all afraid of Le Loup, however, she has no apparent intention of thwarting his schemes," says Kiel.

ELEPHANT WITH ONE LEG MADE OF SAND is the friendly bedfellow of Luxembourg local Alisa, who is five years old.

Elephant with One Leg Made of Sand first made a cameo in one of Alisa's dreams. "Now almost every evening and morning, while she is in bed, she talks to him," says Ekaterina, Alisa's mother. Her bed is their "friendly place." Ekaterina says that Alisa liked our picture, and chose this opportunity to reveal that the elephant is actually a girl.

FALCOR is a bipedal dog who lives in California but commutes to Pennsylvania to see his three-year-old friend Mira.

"Falcor doesn't like lemons and apples, and his favorite thing to do is draw himself," explains Mira's mother, Laura. To date, Falcor has been living in the golden state with his friend Leola, who sometimes joins him on his trips, but Mira recently announced that he is planning to move in with the family soon. "I'm not sure how I feel about that," says Laura.

RIGOBERTA is a fashion-forward llama and friend to six-year-old Martina, who lives in Santander.

Rigoberta first arrived at Martina's home to seek new opportunities because her wool had become fashionable in Spain. Recently, she has been traveling a lot. "First to London, where she has some cousins, and then to Amsterdam, where she has started a special socks brand for riding bikes," says Pati, Martina's mother. Rigoberta liked Amsterdam so much that she now spends half her time there (Martina's father also happens to live in the city).

FEATHERKNIT is a Siberian tiger. She lives between Russia and Sheffield, where she is "tiger mother" to five-year-old Arthur.

"That's my tiger mother!" said Arthur, when his mom Catherine showed him this image. Featherknit is often out rescuing people in the Sheffield area, and keeps up her energy by eating both meat and wild heather. "He said that she's also been in a few accidents, one involving a volcano and lava, and also she has hurt her paw after falling from a roof," says Catherine. Get well soon!

GRANDAD OTIS lives in London. He has been a surrogate grandparent to four-year-old Juno since the start of the pandemic.

Grandad Otis first appeared at a time when Juno couldn't see her real grandparents because of COVID-19. Now that restrictions have lifted he has gone on a beach holiday in South America. Sarah, Juno's mom, got her first glimpse of what Grandad Otis looks like when they went to an art exhibition and Juno pointed to the figure in Jean Debuffet's 1947 painting *D'hôtel* and said "That's him!"

Part 4:
TITBITS

107 — 120

001

Shelf Life

Neda Toloui-Semnani is an Emmy award-winning writer and producer. Her first book, *They Said They Wanted Revolution*, untangles her parents' involvement in the Iranian Revolution and the impact it had on her life. *Publishers Weekly* called it, "an intimate and vital study of the Iranian diaspora."

002

Pass it On
Neda Toloui-Semnani

In early 2022, Neda Toloui-Semnani published *They Said They Wanted Revolution: A Memoir of My Parents*. The book charts her parents' involvement in the Iranian revolution, her father's execution by the state and her mother's escape over the border with three-year-old Neda. Now a mother to an 11-month-old son and living in Brooklyn, she reflects on what lessons she learned from her extraordinary upbringing.

KINDLING: In the first chapter of your book, you ask the question "When does a family begin?" Have you come to an answer?

NEDA TOLOUI-SEMNANI: Sometimes I take comfort in the idea of fate—that my parents were moving toward each other and that everything that came after was meant to be. Although, in the book, I talk a lot about choices. There is a miraculous element to my own experience of becoming a mom. Out of all of the little spirits, I got this one. But there's an inevitability about it too.

K: Your parents' stood by their convictions, even when it put them at great risk. What lesson have you taken from them?

NTS: I don't think anyone deserves every part of you. Once we were living in the US, my mom was somehow able to keep a part of herself from me

and my brother and I think that that became very important to her. I guess the caveat is that my son is 11 months old and I'm sure this will get harder as he gets older, but I have to show him that you don't lose yourself because somebody else needs you. You don't stop living your life because someone else has entered it.

I also think that being firmly middle-aged when I had my first child made that feel very clear to me. I've taken the things that I believe in about myself, that I think helped me get through my life, and put them into a little kernel inside of myself that nobody can get to because I have worked very hard to become that person.

K: Have you thought about what role Iran will play in your son's life?

NTS: I hope that he can go while we still have people there who knew both my parents. The separation between Iran

and the US, it's profoundly sad for those of us who are caught on one side or the other. I haven't seen some members of my family for 20 years. My cousin just had her baby two weeks ago, so our boys are less than a year apart. We're going to make sure they spend summers together or go on holidays together, which is what my mom made sure I did as a child.

K: What have you understood differently about your parents since becoming a parent yourself?

NTS: I was always very confused when people would say that, when I was born, my dad changed. He became besotted with me—that was the word people used. And I didn't really understand what that meant and why that was a big deal—how having a child can soften you and change you and deepen your wells of empathy and joy and love. I spent the first 40 years of my life trying to figure out what it means to be someone's child and I expect I'll spend the next 40 years trying to figure out what it means to be someone's parent.

K: What's one small thing you've replicated from your childhood with your son?

NTS: My mom used to sing this one song to wake us up sometimes and without even thinking about it I've started to do that for my son. I don't know why, but it feels important. **k**

003

Kids Draw Things
Elephants

OLIVER
FIVE YEARS OLD
OREGON, USA

004

Drawings from our Community
@kindlingmagazine

Many modern artists collected works by children because they admired the naïve style, including Picasso, Kandinsky and Matisse. One day, visiting an exhibition of children's art, Picasso said: "When I was their age I could draw like Raphael, but it took me a lifetime to learn to draw like them."

This issue, we asked *Kindling* readers to send us their children's depictions of elephants and received drawings from across the globe including Tasmania, Croatia, Puerto Rico and Indonesia. Thank you for your beautiful and incredibly varied creations—we're only sorry we couldn't print all of them!

Kids Draw Things

Elephants

FRANCES
EIGHT YEARS OLD
WASHINGTON, USA

006

My Time

*My Seline von
Appen Keller*

My Seline von Appen Keller lives in Copenhagen with her husband, Christian, and their four children. In 2017, she founded the children's clothing company Co Label. Here, she talks about how she makes time for herself—and what she does with it.

KINDLING: Your children range in age from five to 12. What do your evenings look like?

MY SELINE VON APPEN KELLER: We put the kids to bed at the same time. They go to bed no later than 8 p.m.—my oldest daughter, she'll read in bed—and we go to bed at 10 p.m. So we have two hours that is just for me and my husband.

K: Is time away from home important to you?

MSVAK: I'm really social. Chris doesn't really crave gatherings as much as I do, so it would mainly be me going out and seeing my friends or to work situations—although luckily my work and my friends are basically the same. If you asked us to dinner, it would be with one of us. We wouldn't go together.

K: Are you good at spending time alone?

MSVAK: This is hard to say, but a year ago I started losing my hair and I got really tired. Because I was always being productive: If I had free time, I would always do dishes or clean or *something*. But really, if there's five or seven laundry baskets, it will not change much.

K: What was the solution?

MSVAK: Idle time, where you don't do anything. Now, if I have an hour or even 20 minutes between something I just sit down. I'm getting really good at not thinking about anything.

K: What are you currently reading?

MSVAK: I used to read a lot of literature. But it makes you *feel* so much and sometimes you just don't want to feel everything all the time. It sounds so corny, but at the moment I'm listening to a lot of podcasts about true crime. It's far from my reality, so I don't feel it in the same way.

K: Denmark has strong social provisions. Does that make it easier to have children and an independent life?

MSVAK: Yes—we have really good maternity leave and we have really good daycare, school and after-school systems. We have a lot of freedom. **k**

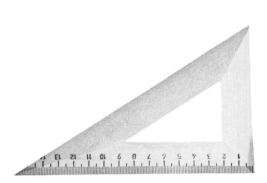

007

Note From Teacher
Liz Kleinrock

Q: What is a respectful way to challenge something on the curriculum?

A: I think many adults have had an experience with one of their choices at work being questioned. How that's approached is going to greatly affect the way we receive feedback or questions. So, storming into the classroom unannounced is going to quickly erode your relationship with your child's teacher.

The first thing I would suggest doing is taking a deep breath and approaching the situation with curiosity. What about the curriculum isn't sitting well with you? Are you supportive of the content, but nervous about how the teacher will deliver it? How might your own identity and experiences be shaping the lens through which you view the curriculum? Second: Do not engage over email. We become less respectful behind a keyboard compared to when we're looking someone in the eye. Request a meeting, and give the teacher a general idea of what you'd like to discuss. Cryptic emails

asking for meetings without a stated purpose stress many people out!

When it's time to meet, remember that criticizing the teacher is not the same as criticizing the curriculum. Thank the teacher for meeting with you and begin by stating your observations, pointing to specific pieces of the curriculum. Again, approach the conversation with curiosity by framing questions such as, "I'm curious about the decision to include this book, can you talk me through it?" or, "Can you tell me about the ways you support students who struggle with this content?" State your concerns and your reasoning behind them.

At this point, if you feel like you have reached a common understanding, you can discuss the next steps to help you (and most likely other caregivers) stay in the loop about what's happening in class. If you are unable to reach a place where you feel comfortable, suggest looping in the principal or another administrator to have a follow-up conversation. **k**

008

Shelf Life

Liz Kleinrock is the anti-bias and anti-racist educator behind Teach and Transform. Her first book, *Start Here, Start Now, A Guide to Antibias and Antiracist Work in Your School Community*, is full of personal stories, sample lessons and resources to help other educators get started with cultivating an anti-bias and anti-racist classroom. She also sits on *Kindling*'s editorial board!

009

Open Here in Case of Emergency
Emma Scott-Child

1. DINNER DEBATE
If you've run out of interesting questions to ask about each others' days, try a dinner debate. Split into teams and make a statement, then argue for or against it using facts, personal evidence or stories based on total nonsense for comic value. It could be simple: *Cats are better than dogs,* or *summer is better than winter.* You could get controversial: *Education is useless!* or opt for the downright weird: *Lost socks are stolen by ghost dogs… Discuss!*

2. EXQUISITE CORPSE
No one was murdered in the making of this game. Exquisite Corpse is a parlor game allegedly invented by drunk Surrealists in the 1920s. Fold a piece of paper into four strips. The first person draws a head on the top strip, the second person—without looking at the previous drawing—draws a torso, the third draws the legs and the fourth draws the feet. *Et voilà,* you've created a surreal beast and—according to André Breton—"liberated the mind's metaphorical activity" all in five minutes.

3. READ MY LIPS
See if you can give someone instructions by mouthing the words to them. If they do the right thing, then they get to take a turn mouthing. You'll soon realize that "clap your hands" also reads a lot like "slap your ass."

4. TONGUE TWISTERS
For maximum adorableness, teach small children tongue twisters and watch their facial expressions as they try to say the words. A personal favorite is quite an easy one: A noisy noise annoys an oyster but a noisier noise annoys an oyster more!

5. PAPER PLINTH
This is a staple assignment for foundational design courses worldwide because it is so simple but offers a huge variety of possible outcomes. Take a piece of letter-size paper and see how much weight it can hold when lifted off the ground. You can fold it into any shape to make it strong and rigid. See if you can make it hold a can or a book.

010
Kids Draw Things
Elephants

ARLO
FOUR YEARS OLD
CALIFORNIA, USA

012
Shelf Life

Emma Scott-Child is a UK-based
creative director and sits on
Kindling's editorial board.
Her 2019 book *Quick Crafts for
Parents Who Think They Hate Craft*
features 40 simple art projects
that don't require lots of
equipment or an hour-long clear
up, allowing you to get creative
with your children even if you're
short on time (or patience).

011
YouTube Corner
Recommendations from our readers

Oscar, from Sydney, says that footage of
planes landing in storms captivates the whole
family. "Our one-year-old gives a hearty round
of applause when each new plane appears
and again when they land, while our three-
year-old has more vim for missed landings,"
he says. Search "Unbelievable Crosswind
Landings" for more.

CLASSIFIEDS

YOU CAN'T BUY THIS KINDLING HAT... YET!

No. 01
Tinycottons:
Summer Style

Tinycottons' imaginative, comfortable clothes are designed to be passed down. This dress comes from the Tiny Islands collection, which is inspired by the sunny colors of a Mediterranean holiday. 2022 marks a decade in fashion for the Barcelona-based company—happy anniversary! *tinycottons.com*

No. 02
Mini Monroe:
Playful Playsuits

Mini Monroe's bright playsuits are made by a Jamaican Swedish family business helmed by designer Vanessa Ford, who makes clothes with her three fun-loving kids in mind. This super-soft Jumpsie is made in small batches in Portugal, where the family is based. *minimonroe.com*

No. 03
Wellipets:
Frog Boots

Since the 1980s, Wellipets has delighted both young and old with its unique designs. Now, the British heritage brand is relaunching its iconic Frog Boot. These wellington boots, which are made in Italy, have shod royalty—princes William and Harry wore them as children. *wellipets.com*

TURN TO PAGE 72 TO LEARN MORE ABOUT CAS HOLMAN'S TOYS!

No. 04

Connetix:
Building Blocks

Connetix magnetic tiles are perfect for building and exploring open-ended play. Featuring strong magnets and a unique bevel design, Connetix easily connect together to form 2D and 3D shapes. Children can explore their imagination, creating their own designs, or follow pre-existing patterns—including this vibrant rainbow. *connetixtiles.com*

Kids Draw Things
Elephants

TEÓ
NINE YEARS OLD
BUDAPEST, HUNGARY

Good Day / Bad Day
Billy Jack Brawner

Billy Jack Brawner is a creative director, previously with *Magnolia Journal*. He lives in New York with his boyfriend Xanthi and has five children, aged between 11 and five, with his former partner, now best friend, Sara. Here, he shares what a good day and a bad day look like for their eight-strong family.

GOOD DAY:
I have a theory that if we're having a really great time doing something and we've been there for a little bit, we should call it quits. We went ice skating last winter and it was so fun. We were there for an hour and a half and I was like "Okay, we should leave!" Everyone gets hot chocolates and we end on a good note. But I think, really, that the adults in our family determine when it's a good day based on whether we're not taking ourselves too seriously. There are moments when it's like "Well, that was kind of magical, the way I handled that situation." Like one time the kids were hot, so we bought a pack of ice and I put it down their shirts and they did it back to me. After that, sure, maybe we're still hot but we're laughing. That's as opposed to the other me who is like, "Yeah, it's summertime. It's going to be hot!" There are lots of moments when I struggle, and I have to come to them and say, "I wish I had done it this way instead." I sometimes think getting it wrong the first time and making up for it is even better.

BAD DAY:
With five kids, it's so easy for one little thing to happen that ruins everyone's fun. Like we'll be out walking and then a kid's shoe is a little too small so they're getting a blister, or someone needs the bathroom and there are no public restrooms and it's like, *Good god, what are we doing!* We used to live in Texas and now we're adjusting to New York where everything is so much more expensive. Recently, after the kids' holiday show, we decided to go for a nice dinner out. I'd given everyone the talk: "People don't think that kids can come to this kind of restaurant and we're going to prove them wrong." Then the kids start acting up, and one kid starts throwing up all over me, then all of the other kids start making a big deal about it. It's a small place full of rich, snooty people. I had to just take him home. The kids didn't enjoy it. We didn't enjoy it. And it was a $400 meal! When things go wrong, they're more expensive for a big family. **k**

015

Five Things That Help
Laia Aguilar

Laia Aguilar lives in the Spanish countryside with her husband and two children, aged 16 and 12. A former advertising director turned kids' fashion powerhouse, she is the co-founder of Bobo Choses and The Animals Observatory. Over the years, every family builds up a unique and often strange repertoire of shared rituals and routines—here, Aguilar shares some of hers.

2. To shake up our routine when the children were younger, we used to go for a walk as a family, usually in the woods. While walking we would name the plants—not by their real name (which many times we didn't know) but by their appearance. For example, the oak tree is called "Torpón" which means clumsy in Spanish, and flowering mimosas are "SpongeBobs."

4. From time to time, when the children were little and we saw that they were having a hard time or that they were too tired and it was a school day, me and my husband pretended we had overslept. So we wouldn't wake them up and we would let them sleep as long as they needed to. To be clear, it wasn't a routine thing!

1. To help my son get to sleep when he was a baby, I used to let him wrap his hand around my hair and tug, tug, tug… This was one of my tricks that worked all the time!

3. To discover new food we go to restaurants as a family and order dishes that we don't know, without thinking too much about it. There are always some good surprises and some not-so-good ones.

5. To decompress we have a family routine: play loud music and dance in the dining room, all together. During the confinement caused by COVID-19, we did it every day. It was a way to enjoy music, to get us moving and, ultimately, have fun and feel happy. Dancing is pure happiness.

016
Stockists
A — Z

A

Arket
ARKET.COM

Bobo Choses
BOBOCHOSES.COM

Christian Wijnants
CHRISTIANWIJNANTS.COM

Closed
CLOSED.COM

Co Label
COLABEL.DK

Connetix
CONNETIXTILES.COM

Crocs
CROCS.COM

Egg Trading
EGGTRADING.COM

Essentiel Antwerp
ESSENTIEL-ANTWERP.COM

Ganni
GANNI.COM

Jelly Mallow
JELLYMALLOW.COM

Jil Sander
JILSANDER.COM

Mini Monroe
MINIMONROE.COM

Mini Rodini
MINIRODINI.COM

Paperchase
PAPERCHASE.COM

Selfridges
SELFRIDGES.COM

Sunchild
SHOPSUNCHILD.COM

Tiny Cottons
TINYCOTTONS.COM

Wellipets
WELLIPETS.COM

Wynken
WYNKEN.CO.UK

017
Credits
Issue 3

STAY IN TOUCH AT @KINDLINGMAGAZINE

P.20
FROM THE CRADLE
*92% of U.S. 2-year-olds
have online record,* C|net,
2010 Share With Care,
Nominet, 2016

PETS AND PASSWORDS
*Sharenting: Children's Privacy
in the Age of Social Media,*
UF Law Scholarship
Repository, 2017

LIKE AND SUBSCRIBE
*10 facts about Americans
and YouTube,* Pew Research
Center, 2019

42%
*Civility, Safety & Interaction
Online,* Microsoft, 2019

72%
*Parents on Social Media:
Likes and Dislikes of
Sharenting,* National
Poll on Children's Health,
2015

31%
*Parents and Social
Media,* Pew Research
Centre, 2015

P.23
Getty Images

PP.28–34
Hair and Makeup: Una Ryu

PP.36–47
Photography assistant:
Victor Pare
Groomer: Sammy Jackson
Models: Jessica and Elizabeth
at KIDS LONDON

PP.52–63
Hair and makeup:
Lisa Zomer

018

Ducks in a Row

Sarah Hingley